blessings

a children's book for grown-ups

Jan Elkins with Anna Elkins

Listening Heart
PO Box 509
Jacksonville, OR 97530 USA
ISBN-13: 978-0-578-43698-2

Cover design & illustrations by Anna Elkins

Printed in the United States of America

Dedication

I dedicate this book of blessings to our children, Anna and David, and to all our spiritual sons and daughters. May these blessings be your inheritance.

Also by These Authors

Jan Elkins and Linda Sattgast:

Teach me about God
Teach me about Jesus

Jan Elkins with Anna Elkins:

A Book of Blessings
Blessings for Love and War
Blessing of Hope and Joy

Anna Elkins:

The Heart Takes Flight
The Honeylicker Angel
The Space Between
And: The Story of More

Table of Contents

Introduction by Anna Elkins

Once upon a time, my mom told me she wanted to write children's blessings inspired by the ancient text, Song of Songs. I had helped with her book, *Blessings for Love & War*—with its blessings for love inspired by Song of Songs. This new idea intrigued me.

What you hold in your hands is a kind of adaptation: we distilled the heart of the scriptural love songs into blessings that both children and grown-ups can receive. Think of this as a children's book for grown-ups.

We wanted people of any background to enjoy these blessings, so we used names for the divine like Beloved, Love, and Friend.

Mom also asked me to illustrate this book. In keeping with the simplicity of the blessings, I drew simple, black-and-white sketches. Whether you are young or eternally young, you are invited to color them. And since many of the lines are "open ended," there is no worry about coloring outside the lines. In fact, I encourage you not only to color outside the lines, but to draw your *own* lines—you'll find plenty of white space to enter into the blessings.

That is the spirit of this book: that you personally experience the heart of Love for yourself.

Enjoy!

Introduction by Jan Elkins

My friend, Jessica, is the mother of five children. When her son Zeke was about two years old, she read to him from *A Book of Blessings*. One week, while Jessica was sick, Zeke came up and kissed her and said, "I bless you mommy for your body to get better."

When she told me this, she added, "You are leaving a legacy with these blessings!"

Other parents have told me similar stories about reading blessings to their children, and so Anna and I were inspired to create a book with shorter blessings that would be easier for little ones to hear—while still being relevant to the "grown-ups."

All the blessings in this book are inspired by the Scriptures. A blessing can be spoken as a prophetic word of encouragement, a declaration, a promise, or a proclamation. A blessing is an impartation of God. When we bless someone, we are taking the living words of God and speaking them into a person's life. God's words are alive and powerful. When read or spoken, His Word shifts the spiritual and physical environment (Hebrews 4:12).

This collection of blessings follows the greatest of love poems, Song of Songs. In it, the Shepherd King—the Beloved—sings His song of passion for His Bride, the Church. It is a divine romance of true love and a prophecy of Jesus the Messiah.

In writing these blessings, I was inspired by multiple sources. One was *The Passion Translation*: *Song of Songs—Divine Romance*. Translator Dr. Brian Simmons describes Song of Songs as an anointed allegory—a divine parable—of how Jesus makes His Bride (the Shulamite) beautiful and holy by casting out her fear with His perfect love. Because the original Hebrew text was written almost three thousand years ago, Dr. Simmons chose to translate the equivalent meaning of the words, not just the words. The name Shulamite and the name Solomon are the same root word—one feminine, one masculine. In essence, all God's people are the Bride, and Jesus the Messiah is the Bridegroom.

Some Bible translations say that Song of Songs is mainly about a marriage of two people made "one flesh" (Genesis 2:24). But translating this text in the context of human marriage provides only a faint image of the unity between God and the soul becoming "one spirit" (I Corinthians 6:17).

The Passion Translation captures the true essence of this allegory. Dr. Simmons' translation truly opened up the most beautiful love story in all the books of the Bible. The parable of Solomon and the Shulamite and their Bridegroom King is the story of my journey and your journey. I have been deeply impacted by this divine poem of romance. I was also inspired by the insight and wisdom in *Song of the Bride,* by Jeanne Guyon. She lived from 1648 to 1717 and influenced the Church mightily. Simmons and Guyon not only gave me a wealth of understanding for Song of Songs, but—more importantly—a love for this ancient book. I incorporated what I learned from those authors into these blessings, including a few explanatory notes at the start of each chapter.

May you be blessed by these blessings.

+   +   +

I used the following Scripture translations while writing:

The Message
The Passion Translation
The Spirit-Filled Life Bible
The New American Standard

CHAPTER ONE

Song of Songs 1:2

The basis for all love is a covenant love. We experience Love's embrace in our spirit and soul where the affections of our heart, our understanding of life, our memories, and our will reside.

The Hebrew phrase that translates into English as "kisses of the mouth" refers to a divine Spirit-kiss: the divine kiss of Love. The original words translated as a "drink of wine" and "kisses" are nearly the same; both express being under the influence of love. Interestingly, "a divine Spirit-kiss" also can be translated as "to equip" or "to arm for battle." We need an impartation of God's Word breathed into us to call us to life and to love. We need His Word to become trained and equipped warriors—overcomers.

Song of Songs 1:5

"Dark as the tent curtains of Kedar" is a wordplay for a "dark place" or a wandering nomad, deeply sunburned from many days exposed to the harsh sun and dryness of the desert. This was the name of one of the sons of Ishmael and represents our old life (Psalm 120:5).

Song of Songs 1:11

Our beauty is enhanced by having been in God's presence and reflecting His glory. "We" is plural for the Trinity.

Song of Songs 1:13-14

This verse describes a bundle of myrrh placed over the heart. When Song of Songs was written, myrrh was used as an embalming spice and was associated with suffering.

The vineyards of Engedi, or the "fountain of the lamb," is an oasis near the Dead Sea with rich vegetation because of its warm springs. Henna, which symbolizes "atonement or redeeming grace" is a small thorny shrub, with beautiful white flowers that hang in fragrant clusters.

Blessing of Divine Kisses

1:1-2

Be blessed
with the breath of the Spirit—
a divine Spirit-kiss—
living words of life.
Catch Love's kisses.

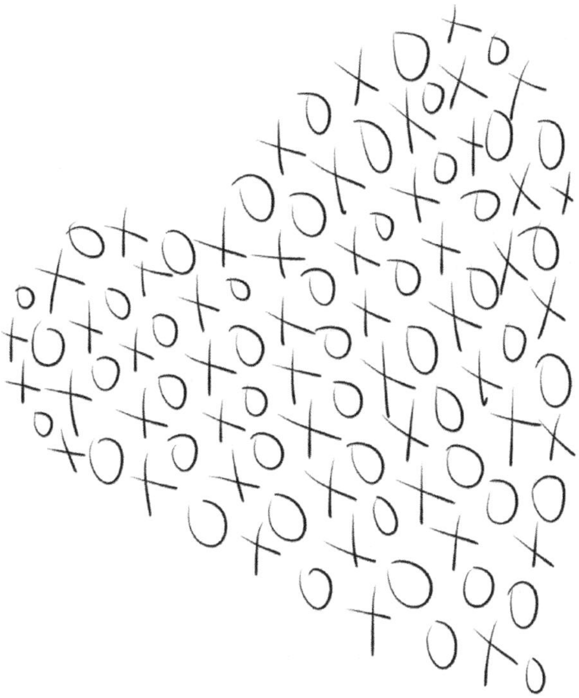

Blessing of Sweetness

I:2

Be blessed with the
sweetness of Love.
Can you taste it?
It's the flavor of kindness,
of saving love,
of forgiving love,
of embracing love—
of love sweet as honey.

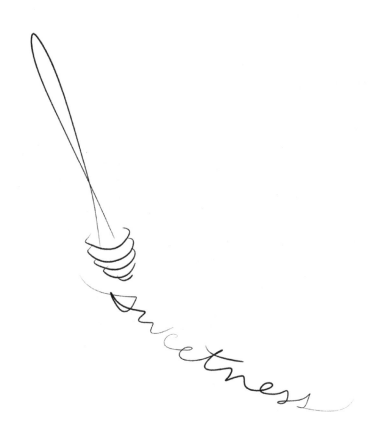

Blessing of a Warrior

I:2

Be blessed with a kiss
of the Spirit to equip
you to overcome.
This kiss of His Word,
makes you ready to move
at the sound of His voice.
May you become a warrior
armed with His heart of love,
His words of hope,
His weapons of truth.

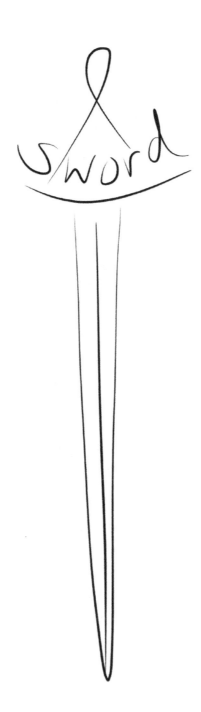

Blessing of Song

I:2

May your heart
be blessed with song.
Sing as you seek,
and sing as you find.
Sing in the dark,
and sing in the light.
Sing when you fall,
and sing as you climb.
Sing when you hurt,
and sing as you heal.
Make this your song:
Your Love is goodness
and more goodness.

Blessing of Joy

1:3-4

Be blessed with joy
in your Beloved.
May this be your song:
I love your presence!
You are Flowing Love—
over me–through me,
curing my wounds,
filling me with joy.
Draw me to you,
and I will follow you.
Together, we will run
to the holy heights.
With you, I can
reach the summit.

Blessing of Grace-Strength

1:5-6, 8

In the dark,
where it hurts,
when it's hard,
and you have wandered,
listen to your Beloved say:
Yet, you are so lovely to me.
As you hear those words,
be blessed with strength
of Grace: Grace-Strength.

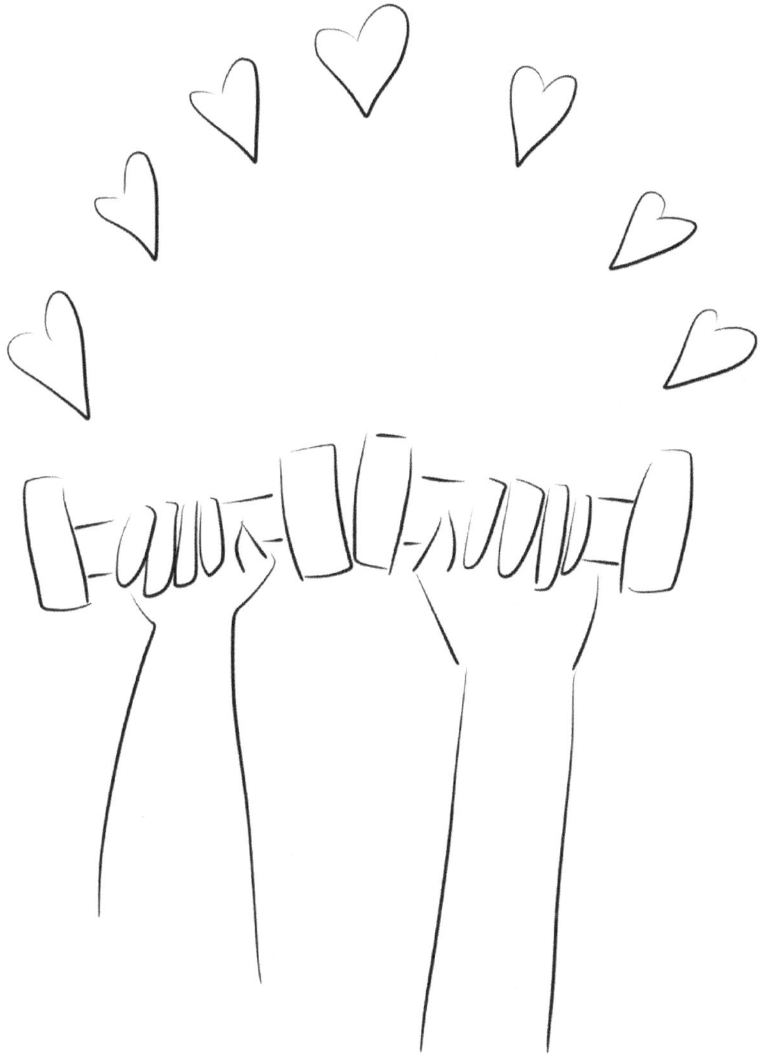

Blessing of Rest

1:6-7

Be blessed with rest.
When the day is hard and long,
when the pressures build
and the problems stack,
when no one listens
and all you hear is hurt,
when the center won't hold
and neither will your heart—
be still.
In the heat of the day
and the heat of the fray,
rest in the cool shade of Grace.

Rest

Blessing of Healing

I:7

Do you have a broken bone?
May its cells reunite in strength.
Do you have a broken thought?
May you create a new one.
Do you have a broken heart?
May it mend in Love.
Listen to your Healer:
If you lose sight of me
just follow in my footsteps,
and I will lead you.

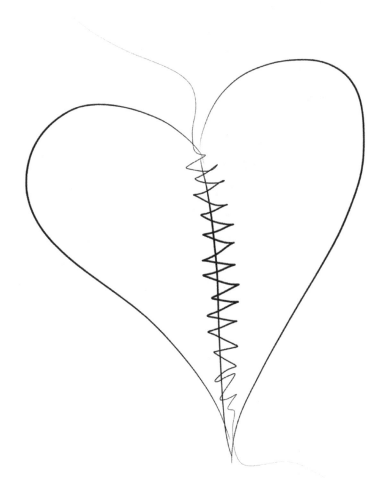

Blessing of Beauty

1:8-11

May you hear the words
of your Beloved:
Radiant one,
bring your cares to me,
bring your burdens to me.
Come to me and you will find me.
Let me show you how I see you.
To me, you are loveliness.
You wear the beauty mark of grace.

Blessing of Transformed Suffering

1:12-13

You are cherished by Love—
may you know it.
You are wrapped in Grace—
may you know it.
Your Beloved has heard
your calls from the dark of night,
having known such night.
Your suffering is not lost
but transformed—your praise
in the pain turns to fragrance
like myrrh suffusing the dark.

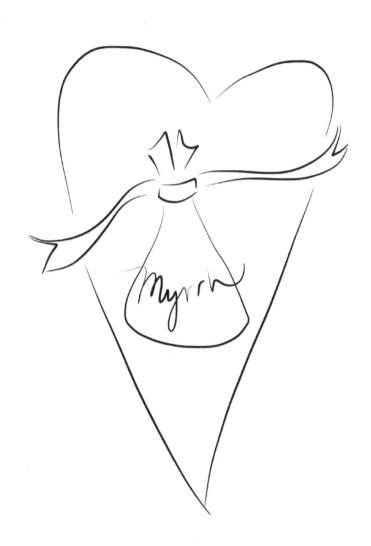

Blessing of Redeeming Grace

1:14

Be blessed with Grace—
surprising Grace,
redeeming Grace.
Grace like a bouquet
of henna blossoms picked
from the vineyards of Engedi.
Breathe in the fragrance
of redemption.

Blessing of Receiving

1:15

May you receive these words
from your Shepherd-King:
My lovely one,
when I look into your eyes,
I see you see me—
I see you receiving my love.
To me—you are beauty itself.

Blessing of True Home

1: 16-17

Be blessed with your True Home—
full of pleasing places to rest,
like a meadow glade in afternoon light,
surrounded by protective trees,
surrounded by peace and delight—
a perfect Home!

peace

delight

CHAPTER TWO

Song of Songs 2:1-2

The root word for "rose" can mean "overshadowed, surrounded, covered." The name "Sharon" can be translated as "His song." You are the theme of His song. A thorn bush points to the curse of sin. A crown of thorns represents the curse of sin being placed on Jesus. Lilies represent purity in our inner being.

Song of Songs 2:6-7

The Shepherd-King has to encourage us to remain at rest in His arms. Song of Songs tells of stages of rest, and Jeanne Guyon describes one stage as the initial embrace of the Beloved in the garden of our hearts. His embrace touches and purifies our senses. From this internal, mystical rest, He will then awaken us.

Song of Songs 2:10-11

This passage describes who we are and who we are becoming. As we become focused solely on God, we will learn to no longer fear winter—the winter is past. In Him, the land of eternal spring is linked to summer and autumn. The heat of summer's passionate love does not interfere with the mildness, beauty, fragrance, and pleasure of spring, or the autumn abundance of fruitful grapes on the vine.

We have all gone through many winter seasons. But the Shepherd-King was always there with us. Though we might look barren of foliage and flowers and fruit, our roots are growing deeper and multiplying. From the winter of our souls, we are also being drawn higher, to dwell with Him in the invisible realm, where there is no fear of a winter season.

Song of Songs 2:15-16

These verses describe a journey of the heart that begins by seeking God within, where He dwells in our spirit. We must spend time in that interior place where we encounter Him face to face. In that place, we are able to face ourselves and be healed from our wounded, untrusting hearts. As we see Him more clearly, He begins to fill our view, and we turn away from self-reflection. We turn away from and beyond ourselves, seeing less and less of ourselves, because we are seeing more of Him.

Song of Songs 2:16-17

The "mountain of spices" means the realm of holiness.

Blessing of Identity

2:1

You are Love's song—
you are the Rose of Sharon.
As you grow in the valley,
may you blossom in the cooling
shade of peace that stretches
across the heat of your days,
tended by Love.

Blessing of Purity

2:2

Listen to the words
of the One you love:
You have been forgiven.
You blossom among the thorns—
in the temple of your inner being,
you have been washed clean
and made pure as a lily.
You are my companion
and dear friend.

Blessing of Delight

2:3

May your spirit fill with delight.
May these words be your story and song:
My Beloved, you tower above all others.
I sit under the shade of your favor;
living in your protection,
blossoming in your presence.
I savor the sweetness of your delicious fruit—
your overwhelming love for me.
I rest with pleasure
where your glory glows.

Blessing of Banqueting

2:4-5

You are invited to the banqueting table
in the Kingdom of Love, Joy, and Peace.
May longing for your King increase—
increasing your capacity to contain more.
Feast on His abundance.
His banner over you is love.

Blessing of Revival

2:4-5

Your Beloved invites you
to the House of Wine—
the home of joy—
to enjoy each other.
Drink of Spirit-wine.
Be revived and refreshed
with promise.

Blessing of Mystical Rest

2:6-7

Be born up by Love's
hands and embraced.
Dwell in Love. Listen
to Love's heartbeat for you.
Be blessed with mystical,
sacred rest so that you
rise up—renewed.

Blessing of Joys of Love

2:8-9

Can you hear the happy voice
of your Shepherd-King calling you?
Can you see Him leaping
over mountains toward you?
He is close to you even when you hide,
even when you don't see Him.
This is the One who calls to you.
This is the One who loves you.
This is the One who
blossoms in your heart.

Blessing of a New Day

2:10-11

May you hear your Beloved:
Awaken my dear, my heart.
Rise from your winter sleep.
Turn from your frozen fears.
The time of hiding has gone—
it is now a new day.
You have asked me to come to you,
now hurry to me!

Blessing of Breakthrough

2:11-12

The season has changed—
it is springtime in the Spirit.
Look—because the rains have soaked
the earth, the vines now bloom with life.
The lilacs are purpling
and the cherry trees are pinking.
Listen—the turtledoves coo
a song of awakening,
inviting you to break through.

Blessing of Destiny

2:12-13

It is the season for singing.
The air fills with songs
of awakening and guidance.
Today, your destiny bursts open
with divine plans and purposes.
Now is the time!
Now is the time to blossom.
Each flower's fragrance
wafts the perfume of change.
Breathe it in.

Blessing of Prayer

2:13-14

Hear your Love calling you higher:
My companion, my friend:
rise up and come away with me.
Run with me to the high places
and be hidden in me.
Let me see your face
and hear your voice.
My heart is captured
by your eyes of love.
I love the sound
of your voice in prayer.

Blessing of Vigilance

2:15

To any part of your heart
where you no longer perceive Love—
where you find it hard to believe,
where you are low on vision,
where you are full of fear—
be blessed with Rescuing Love
who says to you:
Together, let's catch any fox of hindrance
sneaking into our vineyard.
Together, let's remove any threat
to your blossoming love.

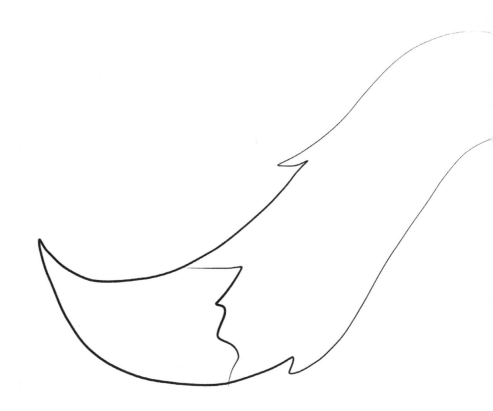

Blessing of Holiness

2:16-17

Even before the new day comes,
chasing away every shadow of fear,
go together now with your Beloved—
ascend to the realm of holiness.
May this be your song:
My Love, I know you are mine
and I have everything in you,
because we delight in each other.

CHAPTER THREE

Song of Songs 3:1-4

These verses tell how the Shepherd-King hides—not out of cruelty but out of love. If He does not "leave," the soul will not seek beyond itself and will never experience what it means to be found in God. A miracle happens in this seeming "absence" of God. So many times, He tenderly invites us to rise up and follow Him. Yet so many times, we settle with the contentment, peace, and tranquility of Him—and we don't want to leave those qualities to follow Him.

Song of Songs 3:5

The second stage of rest refers to a "mystical death"—a dying to self. In this slumber, we receive rest. He calls us to life but also waits for us to choose to awaken and follow Him.

Song of Songs 3:6-11

The Bridegroom King leads the wedding procession in His royal carriage, in a cloud of glory. He has made a mercy seat for those who will become His Bride (the Church).

Blessing of Awakening

3:1-4

May you awaken to your soul's true Love.
If you've been searching for meaning,
if you've been fearing exposure, hurt, loss,
if you've been tossing through sleepless nights—
be blessed with an awakening.
Invite the Shepherd-King to reveal
any secret beliefs that hold you back.
Out of His great love for you,
He will remove them.
He came to redeem you,
He came to form a covenant love with you.

Blessing of the Rest of Heaven

3:2-5

May you know the joy of being known—
may you find when you seek,
be consoled when you suffer,
and be forgiven when you fail.
May you be blessed when you are cursed,
strengthened when you are weak,
and lifted up when you fall down.
May you know the rest of Heaven.

Blessing of Mercy

3:6-11

Look! Your Beloved approaches
in His royal carriage.
He has prepared a love seat for you
under a canopy of mercy.
He is fragrant with redemption,
radiant with strength.
He leads the wedding procession
in a cloud of golden glory.
This is a day of great joy—
a day to celebrate
the beautiful union
of covenant love.

CHAPTER FOUR

Song of Songs 4:6

The "mountain of myrrh" symbolizes suffering love. Love replaces our fears, and that is no easy task. Without love there is only death in our suffering. Though a passionate, true love will involve suffering, that suffering leads to life.

Song of Songs 4:7-8

"The crest of Amana" is translated into English as "amen-Yes" or "faith." It describes the realm where God's promises are securely kept and realized. It is the place where you are seated in the heavenlies.

Song of Songs 4:8

The Shepherd-King describes our open hearts as open halves of a pomegranate—a fruit symbolic of passion (4:3). As we press into His love, we can choose to go with Him to the mountaintop, despite our fears. From that place of heavenly perspective, we can see His blessings of promise. It is from Heaven that we look down upon our circumstances and face our struggles.

What is happening on the outside is not always evidence of what is happening on the inside. In winter, the sap of a tree is not wasted on the externals; all of its energy is focused on extending roots deep into the soil to find the nutrients needed to bud and blossom in the spring. In seasons of dormancy and the cold of winter, we can feel stripped and barren. We have no bright green leaves to cover the defects that have been there all along. But the reality is, the roots of our spirit are going deeper, finding nutrients, and readying for the vibrant and sweet season that's coming.

Song of Songs 4:8-11

The Shepherd-King's impassioned love for you is beyond description. When you struggle with darkness, persecution, betrayal, or disappointment and yet still continue to turn your heart to him, you give Him the greatest gift of love. In eternity, we will be fully devoted to Him; we will see Him fully and worship Him fully. Here on earth, we have the one unique ability to love Him and worship Him in less-than-perfect circumstances. When we worship Him from places of limitation and trials, we touch His heart like no other time.

Song of Songs 4:15

The King pours His life into you—planting, tending, pruning and producing the fruit of His Spirit. His passionate love for you is like the olive, crushed into oil. It is like the grapes crushed into wine. The fruit of the vine He produces in you is also crushed and made into wine, which then flows back into Him, easily taking the shape of His heart.

Blessing of Focus

4:1

May you stay focused
on your Beloved.
Don't break your gaze—
keep this connection.
Listen:
My dear one, my friend,
your eyes are like gentle doves—
I see your devotion
when you look at me.
I see you receive my sacrificial love,
and I see your sacrificial love
offered in return.
To me, you are beauty itself!

Blessing of Pleasure

4:2-3

Hear Love speak:
When I look at you,
I see your passion for me.
When you taste my word,
your life is purified—
you are filled with truth
and mercy and grace.
I see your care for others,
and your heart
brings me pleasure.

truth
mercy
grace

Blessing of Inner Strength

4:4-5

May your soul be secure—
filled with inner strength.
May you focus solely on your
Beloved with pure faith.
May you display grace and love
for Him through your care for others.
May your integrity, honor, and nobility
cause others to surrender
to the strong beauty of Love.

Blessing of Rebirth

4:6

In spite of darkness, shadows, fears—
before the morning comes,
before the promise arrives,
before the full healing—
hope in Love,
be reborn in Love.

Blessing of Exchange

4:6

What if you could swap
sadness for joy,
hidden ills for fulfilled hope,
a "no-way" for a way out,
a "no-win" for a solution?
Give all to the One you love—
exchange the bad for good,
the good for best.
May you decide:
My Love, I've made up my mind.
I will go with you—
yes, I will be yours.

Blessing of Wholeness

4:6

As you face your past, present, and future,
be embraced by Unbroken Love.
May rejection lead to acceptance,
may despair lead to hope,
may regret lead to redemption,
may accusation lead to grace,
may betrayal lead to blessing.
You are made whole in Love.

Blessing of Ascent

4:7-8

May you take heart—listen:
You are now ready, my love.
Come with me—together
we will climb the highest summit,
we will ascend the peaks of Glory,
we will stand in heaven's sanctuary.

Blessing of Yes

4:7-8

Love's promises are *yes*.
Enter the archway of trust,
take hold of heaven's promises
and release them on the earth.
May you say *yes* to the *yes*.

Blessing of Sanctuary

4:8

Your Love—your Healer
& Warrior invites you:
Come with me to our sanctuary.
From there, we will deal with darkness,
betrayal, disappointment, sorrow.
Together, we will fight the very things
that once wounded you.

Blessing of Process

4:8

In the orchard of your heart,
Passion plants, tends,
prunes, and produces fruit.
Passion doesn't always seem active,
but even in the dormant seasons,
when branches look bare,
it sends roots deeper.
Be blessed with character
as you grow in invisible places.
Your winter does not define
your future, but it does nourish
growth for your future.

Blessing of New Life

4:8

Say to your winter: *Spring is here!*
Be blessed with warmth
after shivering in the cold.
The trees in your orchard
now draw up nutrients
collected in dormancy—
sending them up
to bud and blossom across
all that has lain bare.
Be blessed with new life
blooming through the snow.

new life

Blessing of Priceless Beauty

4:8-9

Listen to the Shepherd-King:
With a single glance,
you have undone me with your love.
I am overcome.
You have stolen my heart—
my beloved, my friend.
I am held enraptured by your love
and by the gleaming grace of you.
Like a divine jewel, you are priceless,
shining, and brilliant.

beauty

Blessing of Sweet Words

4:10-11

Be blessed with these words
from your Beloved:
You are so pleasing to me,
my friend, my equal.
Your love thrills me—
it's better than my finest wine.
Your loving words
are sweet to me,
sweet as honeycomb,
fragrant as roses.

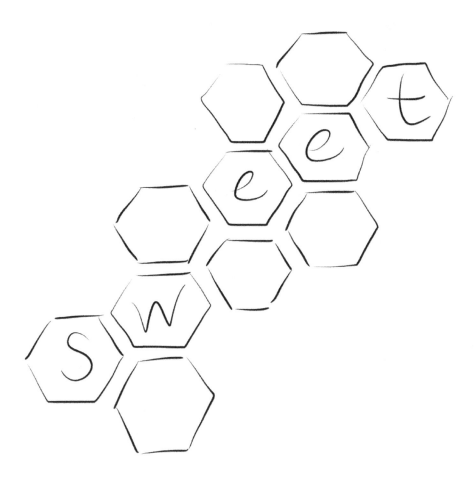

Blessing of a Secret Garden

4:12

Hear your Beloved's song:
I have encircled you with love.
You are a secret garden
only you and I can enter.
You are a bubbling spring,
a fountain of living water.
You are perfect for me.

secret garden

Blessing of Exquisite Fruit

4:13-14

Be blessed with these words
from the Shepherd-King:
Your inner life is a garden of bounty,
growing into a paradise
of promise and presence.
Your tears and my tears
have watered the fruit born here—
fruit of passion,
fruit of mercy,
fruit of redemption,
fruit of healing,
fruit of my suffering love
dripping from Calvary's tree.
Their fragrance envelops you
and the world around you.

Blessing of Wellsprings

4:15

You are pure as a garden fountain
springing from deep wells—
splashing up to sparkle in the sun.
You are like a mountain brook
streaming into the heart
of your Beloved.

Blessing of True Love

4:16

Your True Love kisses you
with the breath of Heaven.
Breathe in Love's words—
rouse dormant dreams from sleep,
stir sleepy passion to life.
Awaken and arise!
May this be your heart's cry:
Come, Spirit wind—
breathe upon me
with your awakening breath.

Arise!

Blessing of Anointing

4:16

Listen for the wind
of the Spirit approaching—
bringing dormant things to life,
stirring up the sweet
fragrance of Life in you.
May you do only those things
He is breathing on.
Receive His anointing
to do great exploits.
Move in a new dimension
of signs and wonders—
be a sign and a wonder.

Blessing of Strength

4:16

Are you tired and exhausted?
Has your breath been knocked out of you?
Have you reached your limit?
Be resuscitated by the breath of the Spirit.
Be blessed with the breath of His Word
releasing supernatural strength.

Blessing of Acceleration

4:16

Be blessed with Love's
breath of refreshing.
Fly with Spirit-wind at your back,
and ride the slipstream of the Spirit,
creating rest and accelerating
into destiny and destination.

Blessing of the New

4:16

Get ready—the new is coming!
Be blessed with alignment
for the new of the Spirit.
Get ready for things to swirl
and shake and shimmy
into a better and brighter fit.
Get ready!

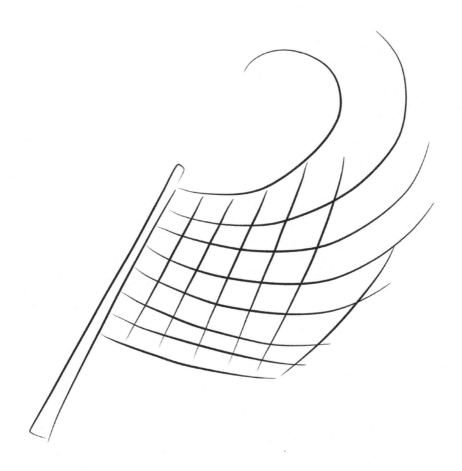

Blessing of Paradise

4:16; 5:1

Your Beloved has come to you—
He walks with you,
He talks with you,
He tastes the fruit of His love in you—
you are His Paradise garden.
May you respond:
Come, Spirit-wind,
with your awakening breath—
spare nothing,
hold nothing back,
until I am fully yours.

CHAPTER FIVE

Song of Songs 5:2-5

The Bride has a troubled dream that her Beloved has left her. But He has only withdrawn from her sight because she delayed responding to His love. This passage also describes Jesus in the garden of Gethsemane praying all night for us. His agony was so great, the sweat on His face appeared as droplets of blood (John 17).

Song of Songs 5:6-8

Sometimes, you think issues in your life are fully dealt with, and then they reappear. Sometimes, you suffer slander, betrayal, dishonor, and persecutions. In such times, you are experiencing death to self-life. You are invited to open your heart deeper to God. He will transform you during what John of the Cross famously called "the dark night of the soul."

Song of Songs 5:11-12

In this passage, the hair/locks black as a raven refer to God's word written in Heaven. Jewish rabbis teach that the precepts of the Torah are written in the heavenly realm with black letters on top of white flames of glory fire.

Blessing of Celebration

5:1

Your Beloved celebrates you
and the fruit of His life in you.
He invites everyone to share
the feast of His life in you:
Come friends—feast on my fruit.
Come, drink until you are full—
until you can take no more.
Take all you desire.
Come, we will all celebrate—
let us raise our glasses
to love and life!

Blessing of Heavenly Dreams

5:2

In the darkness of the night,
may you dream of True Love
knocking on your heart's door,
calling you—
Wake up, rise up!
Will you open your heart
even deeper to me?
Will you receive me?
I have spent myself
this dark night
praying for you.
Will you come away with me?
May you answer, *yes!*

Blessing of Surrender

5:3-4

The One you love is reaching
into your heart for more.
Do you wonder how to respond?
Do you ask: What more can I give?
You are blessed with forgiveness
and cleansing. You have come so far,
yet Love keeps inviting you to unlock
your whole heart. Love longs for more
of you and more for you.
May your spirit awaken
and rise up to meet Love.
May your spirit surrender to Love
and become one heart.

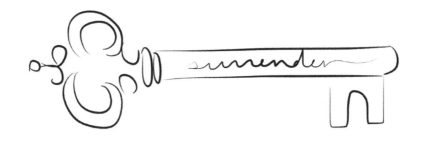

Blessing of Living

5:2-4

Receive Love—and may you
desire to receive even more.
Breathe in the fragrance of suffering love
of the One who knows your sorrows
and carries your pain—
the One who heals you
and brings you back to life.

Blessing of Seeking

5:5-6

In the delays and haste,
in the darkness and hard times,
be blessed with a heart
set on the One you love.
Even when you call out
but can't hear or see anyone,
even when you stumble around
and stub your soul looking,
seek and you will find.

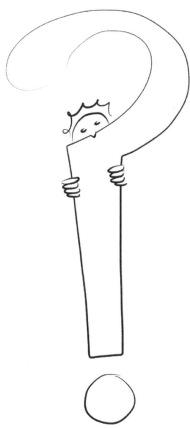

Blessing of Courage

5:6-7

Be blessed with courage to keep
an open heart to Love.
The courage to not hide—
to not be separated
by familiar judgments,
distanced superiority,
vowed self-protection,
illusory independence.
Instead, may you long
for the One who loves you,
who heals all wounds
and deals with all obstacles.
Be blessed with courage
to receive Love.

Blessing of Hope

5:6-8

Be blessed with heavenly hope.
Your Love has been with you
through thick and thin,
through ups and downs,
through back and forths.
In Heaven, hope is a certainty—
secured in the invisible realm,
ready to be made visible.
While you seek,
hold your hope high.

Blessing of Presence

5:6-8

May you know the delight
of the nearness—
the here-ness—
of your Beloved.
Keep close.

Blessing of Rescuing Love

5:8-9

Be blessed with the One
who rescues you,
even from yourself.
Don't turn aside—
be filled with Love,
be spilling out Love
everywhere you go.

Blessing of Holy Desire

5:9-10

May you have such deep
desire for your Beloved
that others will ask of you:
What love is this?
May you answer:
My Beloved is splendor—
no other love can touch my heart
like the Lover of my soul.
This love is Heaven on Earth.

Blessing of the Word

5:11-13

May your spirit be blessed
with wonder for the One
who wears a dazzling crown of glory
embossed with living words.
This glory reflects
on all who come near.
Hear the deep wisdom,
the beautiful insights,
the pure understanding.

Blessing of Light-Filled Beauty

5:13-14

May you be blessed
with the light of Beauty—
light filtered with truth
and glowing with glory,
light anointed with healing,
light illuming revelation,
light bright,
luminous light.

Blessing of Nobility

5:14-15

May all be amazed
by the Incomparable One—
whose heart is a work of art,
whose ways are wise,
whose stance is fixed
whose power is unlimited.

Blessing of the Ineffable

5:16

Some things are so vast
that words cannot express them.
Be blessed with inexpressible
Love—Ineffable Love.
Be free from reasoning through it—
simply receive.
Know the heart of the best Beloved
beating for you in the indescribable
language of Love.

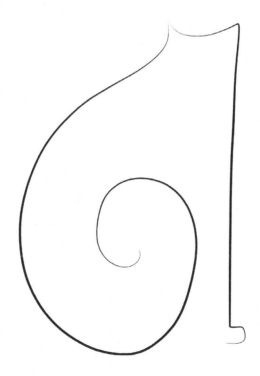

CHAPTER SIX

Song of Songs 6:11-12

The Shulamite goes down to the valley streams where the King's orchards grow and mature. As noble as her intentions are in this passage, she is acting from her own determination—relying on her own influence and persuasion. She longs to know if people are opening their hearts to the King. She finds herself suddenly, lifted up and seated together with the King, no longer focused on herself and her work.

Song of Songs 6:13

This passage references a memorial name in covenant history mentioned in Genesis 32:1-2. The dance of love is literally "the dance of Mahanaim" or "the dance of two armies." As Jacob returned home, a portal of Heaven opened up revealing a gathering of two camps of angels. Jacob named the place Mahanaim, meaning "This is God's camp."

Blessing of Wholeheartedness

6:1

May you give your heart
wholly to your Beloved.
May all half-heartedness
dissolve in the sum of Love
and become one.
May you receive and give
wholehearted Love.

Blessing of Fullness

6:1-3

Where is your Beloved?
In your spirit—
your inmost center,
the garden of your heart,
taking delight in all
you have planted
and tended together.
Be blessed with knowing:
Love is fully yours,
and now you are fully Love's.

Blessing of Overwhelming Love

6:4-5

When overwhelmed by tasks,
be blessed with overwhelming Love.
When consumed by troubles,
be blessed with all-consuming Love.
Listen to your Beloved speak:
I am overcome when I see
the beauty of our oneness.
I am overpowered
by a glance from you.
I am undone by your
devotion to me!

Blessing of Inner Beauty

6:6-9

Love wants you to know:
My truth shines through you—
you are perfect for me.
I see your commitment to me.
I see your love hidden
behind your humility.
Others see your inner joy
and beauty and call you blessed!

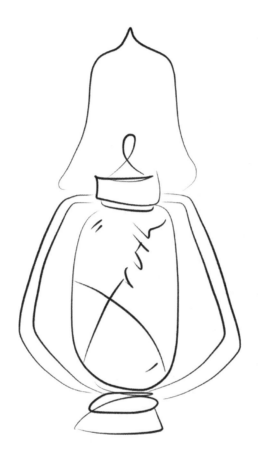

Blessing of Expansive Love

6:9-10

You are blessed by Love
as large as galaxies—but closer.
Love bright as stars—but undying.
Look at you—
growing up like the dawn,
moon-lovely, sun-radiant—
as splendid as the display
of the night sky.

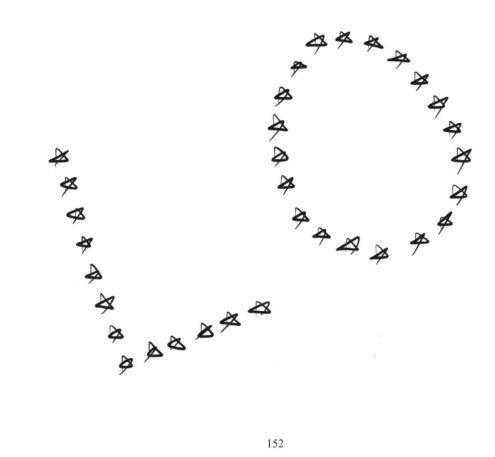

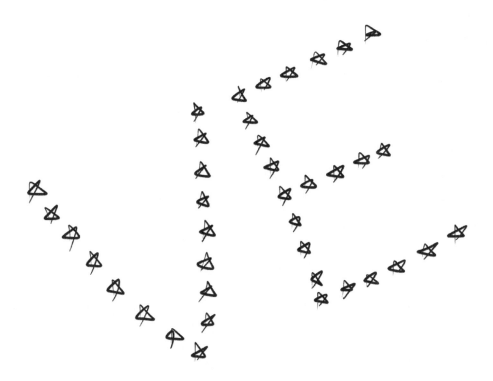

Blessing of Victory

6:10

As you stand beside your Beloved,
armed for every battle, take heart—
you have been made ready.
The banners of victory billow above,
and the foes of fear and sin lie crushed below.
Be blessed with victorious Love.

Blessing of Glory

6:11-12

As you walk along the valley streams
where the orchards of the King grow,
look less for the bloom and fruit
and more for your Beloved.
Together, may you find yourself
lifted up into glory.

Blessing of Dancing Joy

6:12-13

Get up! Leap up!
It is time to dance in joy.
See—even the angels
shimmy in victory.
Accept the invitation.
Twirl out into the flowers—
there are no wallflowers
in this garden. Be blessed
with the joy of dancing.

CHAPTER SEVEN

Song of Songs 7:1-9

Saint Francis de Sales said that the fruit of the vine—wine—is God's beverage. The fruit God produces in us is made into wine, which then flows back into God.

When liquid is poured into a vessel, it easily takes the shape of the vessel, having no form of its own. The soul, however, in its natural, self-willed state, has its own set form; it is obstinate and willful to the point of rigidity. Wood, iron, and stone must feel the fire, the wedge, and the hammer to change their form.

However, a heart that is soft and yielding is called a melted or a liquefied heart. Such a heart can flow into God. Such a heart can be touched and molded by Holy Spirit.

Jeanne Guyon described the soul as having stature like certain palm trees (verse 7). Life-giving water is found where there are palm trees. The female palm has two characteristics. The more fruit it bears, the more upright it becomes. And it will not bear any fruit unless it is under the shadow of the male palm tree.

You cannot perform the slightest action by yourself unless you do all things with the Bridegroom. The fruit you bear will not bend you toward yourself; it will make you stand straighter under the covering of His presence.

Song of Songs 7:11-13

At first, the Bride longs to see if the vineyards are flourishing (6:11). But now, together with the Bridegroom, she runs to the vineyards of His people to see if they are awakened and flourishing (7:11).

Song of Songs 7:12

The pomegranate symbolizes emotion and human passion. It is a "blushing fruit" and speaks of our passion for the One we love.

Blessing of Royalty

7:1

May you rise up into your destiny—
you are true royalty!
You walk with grace and beauty.
The news of Goodness
follows you like a procession.
You are the prize poetry of Love—
a living, moving, masterpiece.

Blessing of Light

7:2-4

May the light of Love
illuminate your heart,
and fill your spirit.
May the light of Love
shine through you,
and reflect from you.

Blessing of Discernment

7:4-5

Redeeming Love blesses you
with strength
with wisdom
with discernment,
with understanding
with clear-sightedness,
protecting you from danger.

Blessing of Bounty

7:6-7

Your Beloved is blessed
with the delicious bounty
from your garden of love.
The love you share abounds—
may you enjoy it together!

Bounty

Blessing of Exhilaration

7:8-9

Your Beloved speaks:
I will bless every part of you.
Your words, like kisses,
wake the sleeping.
I will drink your love like wine.
I will drink your words like wine.
I will drink your kisses like wine.
Love, speak, kiss.
You exhilarate me.

Blessing of Shaping

7:10

May you take shape like clay
in the centering hands of Love.
May you stay soft and pliable.
May you love the form you take—
the form the Potter gives.
May you know that your heart
is filled by Him.
May His desires be fulfilled in you.

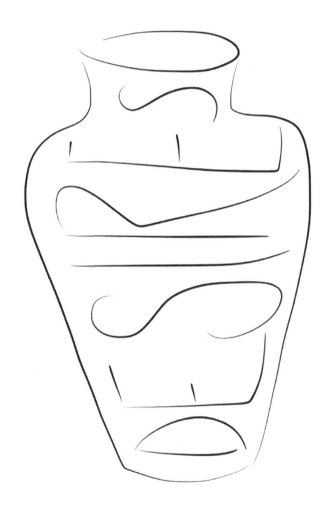

Blessing of Discovery

7:11-12

May your heart speak:
My Beloved, come with me
to see your vineyards,
to see if there are blossoms,
to see budding fruit.
Let us share your goodness with others.
Let us display our passion,
to awaken their hearts.

discovery

Blessing of Fruit

7:12-13

May your heart be a harvest
of the seasons' sweetest fruit.
May love apples fill your trees.
May the blushing pomegranate
yield countless seeds.
Give every good fruit within you—
rare and common,
fresh and preserved—
to your Lover-Friend.

CHAPTER EIGHT

Song of Songs 8:1-2

The Shulamite looks back over her personal history—her upbringing, her mother's instructions, and even as far back as her birth—longing for things to be different. She wishes that her Beloved had been part of her family, like a brother. If he had been a member of her family, no one would despise her love for Him.

Song of Songs 8:3-4

The third sleep of Song of Songs is a state of rest—a lasting place of rest. When we are free from self, we can rest in the freedom to live wholly and fully for God.

Song of Songs 8:5

Although we have a natural birth, we experience a rebirth when the King awakens us. It is a spiritual rebirth—a restoration and return to innocence. We discover our identity—who we belong to and who we are as royalty. He is able to heal as far back as needed, even to our birth; there is no limitation in time or distance in the Spirit.

Blessing of Big Love

8:1

This Big Love you have—
may you be unashamed to show it
and unashamed to share it.
Be blessed with the strength
to give it to those who mock it.
Display the Love
that displaced the dark—
the Love that saved you.

Blessing of Healing

8:1-2

You are made one with your Beloved.
He carries you into your past,
your present, and your future
and heals your hurts along the way.
May you open every part of your heart—
all your family history,
every memory good or bad,
every place of injury,
every place of shame,
and let Perfect Love heal.

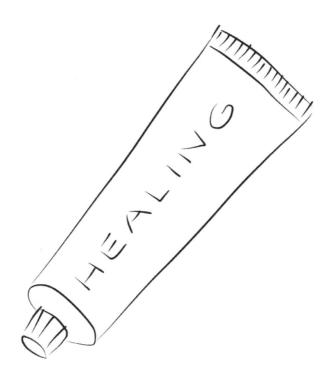

Blessing of a Big Heart

8:2

How much love
can your heart hold?
Try and find out!
Let your heart get bigger
and bigger—surpass
your capacity, fill
to the brim and then spill out.
Be blessed with a big heart
for all the love you'll share.

183

Blessing of Enduring Rest

8:2-4

The barren winter is past—
you are free from its cold grip.
You are secure in the inner sanctuary,
embraced in Perfect Love.
Be blessed with undisturbed,
enduring rest.

Sanctuary

Blessing of Remembrance

8:5

Remember how you walked out
of the desert, arm in arm
with your Beloved—
your sole support.
Look at you now!
He has awakened you to life and love.
Remember to keep feasting on His love,
always longing for more of Him.

Blessing of Consuming Love

8:6

May you be consumed
in the Flame of Love.
May your heart
be sealed in Love—forever.
Love is invincible.
Love faces danger and death.
Love laughs at the terrors of hell.
Love burns through lies
and sparkles with truth.
Love is a firewall of safety
surrounding you.

Blessing of Sacrificial Love

8:7

Listen to Love sing over you:
Nothing can douse my flame of love.
Rivers of miseries cannot put it out.
Floods of distresses cannot drown it.
Nothing can quench my love
that burns within you.
My fire keeps burning
until even suffering turns to pure love,
until all is refined in our Oneness.

Blessing of Protection

8:8-10

May you let Love build
a wall of protection
from self enemies—
self-love,
self-determination,
self-reliance.
And once safe,
may you be a place
of safety for others
so that they, too,
may guard their hearts.
Be blessed with giving
what has been given to you.

Blessing of Oneness

8:11-13

May you know the beauty
of being one with your Beloved—
together in your center,
your heart's garden.
May you always hear
His voice and song of love.

Blessing of a Unified Heart

8:14

Hear the Beloved calling you—
Rise up!
Will you come to me, my beloved?
Will you come dance with me
on the mountains
fragrant with spices,
ever united as one?
May you be blessed with saying *yes*.

Acknowledgements

Thanks to my daughter, Anna. Your life vision of *art + word + spirit* inspired us to offer this divine poem of romance in this format for all age groups. Thank you for partnering with me to reach my goal—that adults and children alike be impacted by the greatest love story of all the ages.

About the Authors

JAN ELKINS and her husband, Garris, worked in the ministry of church planting, pastoring, and overseas missions for decades. Jan's passion has been in the prayer ministry for inner healing. Her desire is that every person be touched, awakened, and transformed by God's immeasurable, extravagant love. She is the author of *A Book of Blessings, Blessing for Love & War, Blessings of Hope & Joy,* co-author of the children's books, *Teach Me About God* and *Teach Me About Jesus.* Jan and Garris have been married for 45 years, and they have two children, Anna and David.

ANNA ELKINS is a poet and painter. She has written, painted, and taught on six continents—publishing a few books and exhibiting many paintings along the way. Her most recent "children's book for grown-ups" is *And: The Story of More.* Anna has set up her writing desk and easel in Southern Oregon.

P.S.

We do hope you'll draw/color/paint/add to this book! If you do, take a photo and send it to us. Email images to Anna at: **ae@annaelkins.com**

Be blessed!

40138101R00110

Made in the USA
Middletown, DE
23 March 2019